Residential Emergency Manager

Francis Gaffney

ISBN: 978-1-365-84136-1

PublishNation LLC
www.publishnation.net

Table of Contents

Chapter 1

Prepare Now, Worry Less

When the term Emergency Management is used, people often think of businesses and local, federal, and state agencies. It is my opinion that the most needed emergency management plan is the one that is in place for your home. Who is responsible for preparing your home? The answer is you, the homeowner.

The title Residential Emergency Manager is a Neologism or new term I have yet to hear in my Emergency Management education. This title encompasses all the duties needed to keep you and your loved ones safe (pets included). These duties include planning for fire protection, storm protection, earthquake protection, security, medical needs, insurance, and any other preparation needed every homeowner or renter should have. Each year storms and other emergencies take the lives of persons all around the world. I believe some of these deaths could have been prevented by planning for the potential threats that a Residential Emergency Manager faces.

Unfortunately, for many Residential Emergency Managers preparation begins too late or not at all. You have a responsibility to your family, your pet(s), and yourself to prepare your residence the best you can. This book will provide you with basic information on what you can do to better prepare. Simple steps that you take could mean the difference between living through an emergency situation and becoming a victim.

I cannot make any guarantees that the information I provide to you in this book will make sure that you are safe in an emergency situation. It is my opinion that by doing nothing and turning to others for assistance, you may be risking your life.

Professional Emergency Managers encourage homeowners to have plans in place. They recognize that the more homeowners prepare, the easier the job they will have in responding to other persons that may be in need.

Weather events are just some of the possible events that could cause an emergency to occur. An earthquake can produce more energy than atomic bombs. Seismologists report seismic activity is increasing and a large earthquake is overdue in many parts of the world. Solar storms could send a large pulse toward earth that would damage much, if not all of the electric grid, sending the homeowner back to a time when electricity was not an option for a period of time.

The power grid in the United States and in many other countries around the world needs updating. Cyber attacks might possibly knock out water supply systems or electric systems, and cause damage that would take weeks or months to repair. A computer virus or worm is difficult to detect and can be nearly impossible to trace. The threats we face from rising tides to terror attacks is unfortunately high and so is the damage that could occur. Populations now occupy areas that were not inhabited or were sparsely populated 100 years ago. The roadways that were designed to evacuate populations were designed many years ago as well. Emergency managers have plans in place to move large populations. However, no plan can address all the possible scenarios that an area might face. You might be on your own for a significant amount of time before help can arrive.

The time to prepare your residence for an emergency is now. When an emergency is predicted, or occurring, it may be too late. I had never really given much thought to preparing my home until Hurricane Sandy struck the state of New Jersey in October of 2012. I was an off-duty Police Sergeant at a very nice small-town municipal police department when the super storm hit. The storm caused massive power outages throughout the northeast. Almost eight million residences and businesses on the East Coast of the United States lost power.

Super storm Sandy resulted in the loss of 48 lives in New York, 12 in New Jersey, 2 in Pennsylvania, 5 in Connecticut, and 5 in other parts of the country. I was home with my family during the storm and lost power minutes after the high winds hit. My son was safe at a friend's house down the road. The winds were forecasted to be high and the weather stations predicted the storm would produce power outages. We had warnings and predictions the storm was coming. Many emergency situations that could occur will not provide any warning.

A year prior to Sandy, in late August of 2011, Hurricane Irene had made its way up the East Coast and caused a power outage that lasted ten days for my neighborhood. I really did not like having no electric for that ten-day period. We had two young children at the time and they were miserable without the everyday items we take for granted when the power is on.

During the outage, I obtained a decent sized generator for a reasonable cost. As soon as I gassed it up and started it, the power came back on. I kept the generator and my first preparation step was taken. I knew I needed to drain the gas out of the tank and carburetor. I had worked for a lawn mower repair shop during college so I was very familiar with gasoline and the need to keep the gas from going bad. I placed gas stabilizer in the stored gas to keep it from going bad as well. I knew I might need it again one day. I was beginning to prepare my home for emergencies, but I had a lot to learn and much more work to do. I did not know it at the time, but I was a Residential Emergency Manager in the making.

I had the generator ready to go prior to Sandy striking and as soon as the power went out, I started it up and kept it running with refueling for the next week. We turned it off at night to keep the noise down in the neighborhood. I was prepared for the power loss. However, many were not, including my neighbor who asked to hook up to my generator. We worked out a deal where I would supply some power and they would share the cost of fuel. Working together during difficult situations is so very important and we are lucky to have great neighbors. Part of preparing is making these agreements prior to an emergency, especially if you have a disability or may require extensive assistance from a neighbor or friend.

After the winds died down, I went to pick up my son who was at a friend's house. What I saw when I looked around the neighborhoods of my town was startling. I could not see a light on for miles in any direction. I drove around trees lying in the road and under wires that were hanging low. The hill that sits to the north of my house is usually well lit with many household lights. It had none. It was an eerie sight to say the least. The damage would take weeks and months to repair. Several years later, many people along the coast are still recovering. My neighborhood was lucky compared to the New Jersey Shore and Breezy Point, N.Y., where 110 homes burned.

A day later I started my scheduled tour at the police department. I left my family with power and was lucky enough that temperatures were not as cold as they could be during October in New Jersey. I arrived at work and realized the borough was starting to recover. However, most of the area was without power. An army of power trucks, as well as outside law enforcement agencies, would soon arrive in the state and begin assisting in keeping the peace and restoring power.

Gasoline was a major issue for New Jersey. Gas rationing started and brought me immediately back to my youth when gas shortages caused rationing at the stations. We did not have any major issues with people getting out of hand, but the tension was definitely high. A plan was put into place by Governor Christie to ration the gasoline distribution. The odd/even rationing relates to who is allowed to fill up depending upon the last digit of the license plate. The lines for refueling were very long and stations would run out of fuel. I never thought that in my police career I would be monitoring gas lines to insure compliance. This was a very real wake-up moment for me in determining that I needed to have better preparations at my home for storms and other emergencies.

I directed traffic for power companies and saw happy faces when power was restored to homes. I also saw the frustration when day after day of no power caused people to become more and more upset. I saw neighbors helping neighbors and heard some stories of thefts of generators and fights in gas lines. I realized few people had generators or some of the basic supplies needed to get through just a few days without power.

I was able to get gasoline as one of the gas stations in town did have fuel and power. First responders were given first access to the gas. This allowed me to get to and from work without any problem. One of the factors that kept people calm was that gas was coming in and was being pumped in several areas. However, the supply was low. Some people drove to Pennsylvania for gas as they had mostly escaped the storm. If the gas was to continue to be of shortage or worse yet, was unavailable in neighboring states, the situation would have become much more dangerous.

One of the calls I was dispatched to was from a concerned family member from out of state that was unable to reach two elderly parents. I went to the house hoping not find anyone deceased, and was met at the door by a happy older couple that explained to me that they had been without power many times before. Books, games, and other items that do not require electricity had kept them busy. Actually, they were enjoying the peace and quiet. I learned a lot from them regarding the need to stay positive when facing a difficult situation. I made contact with the family member and informed him that although they were without phone or power they were in great spirits. Maintaining a positive attitude and making the best of any situation will lessen the stress on everyone. If you have kids they will likely be scared if a power outage occurs. They will look to parents for words of encouragement and a feeling of safety.

Over the course of the next two weeks I realized that super storm Sandy was predicted and still many lives were lost. The winds were intense and the coastal storm surge was high. However, the accumulated rains did not materialize, which would have made the area I lived in and the area I was patrolling much worse.

The assessment I made regarding the status of my preparation is that I had not prepared my residence for the potential threats we faced. I had a lot to learn and am still learning how to prepare for the possibility of losing water, power, and other scenarios that hopefully never occur. We often do not want to think about bad scenarios occurring, but after seeing how poorly prepared I was I knew I needed to protect my family better. The most important thing in the world to me is my family and I would do anything for them. I had not taken some basic, easy steps to make sure they can get through an emergency situation, especially if I was called into work and unable to be at home to assist.

I know I am not alone and many households are in the same position I was prior to Sandy. Some households are not even prepared for the slightest emergency situation. That is scary to think about, especially since many of them have the means to procure the necessary items.

I am a volunteer firefighter and have been in many homes with no smoke detectors or carbon monoxide detectors. These are the most common sense items that houses should have, yet each year people die in fires because someone failed to make a small investment in a smoke detector.

Local, state, and federal personnel will help many people in disaster situations. They are very well prepared and each year train to become better. I urge you to not rely solely upon them. When disasters strike, heroes will be dispatched to help when possible, but the system may become overloaded. Help may not come in time. Whatever preparations you do will make the job of first responders easier. The less time and resources they need to spend on you the more they can spend on others that may be in worse shape.

This book focuses on the homeowner and preparations that can be made in the home or automobile, that will assist in keeping you safer. If you have a home-based business the information may be of assistance as well. The investments that I suggest you make in preparation will be worth it. Hopefully, none of them will ever be needed. No one can guarantee a terror attack, an industrial accident, or natural disaster will not strike in your area. No part of this great country, or world for that matter, is immune from the possibility of catastrophic emergency or disaster. I wish you the best of luck as you begin your preparation or evaluate your current preparation status for areas of improvement.

Chapter 2

Water, Heat, and Food

Water is, in my opinion, the most necessary preparation item and the cheapest item everyone needs in the event a situation occurs that makes getting water not possible. The human body can go weeks without food, but without water, in just a few days death is certain. We often take for granted that we will turn on the faucet and water will come out. When a water main breaks and the water is shut off even for a short time we quickly realize drinking, showering, and brushing your teeth suddenly becomes much tougher. Luckily, these inconveniences are rare and usually quickly repaired. What if the pipes could not be prepared for a much longer time because of an earthquake, tornado, or contamination? Water companies have made great progress toward preparing against terror or breakage events. However, my experience has been that many of the water delivery systems are in need of repair. I have worked overtime details with members of water companies that have advised me some water delivery pipes in my area are very old. Your area may have more updated delivery systems and if so, great, however no company can guarantee the water will always flow.

I keep multiple cases of bottled water in my home at all times. I never allow the stockpile to go below several cases. I have a family of four and a case for each one of us, depending upon conditions, would get us through many emergency situations. I also store water for my dog as he is a vital part of my family. Do not forget your pets when making water calculations. The more water you store the better is my philosophy. Limited space may hamper the quantity.

In the event of water loss for extended periods of time I purchased water purification straws that will allow my family to drink from a stream or other water source that is nearby. The cost of these straws is not unreasonable, however having this item in an emergency kit is essential. I purchased mine at a local store for around ten dollars. The minimal cost is worth the investment and straws can easily be packed into a go bag to be brought with us in the event of an evacuation. I have not tested them to see how the water tastes, but I trust that others have made sure they will work to keep contaminants out. If it comes to the point that I am drinking out of a stream through a straw, I probably will just be happy I am able to drink the water and will care little what it tastes like. Hopefully, this is one investment I never have to use.

For anyone that is on a tight budget water can be obtained from a faucet and stored in a bottle or other suitable container for long periods of time. It is essential to start with a clean bottle and make sure you store it in a place that is out of the light. A tight seal keeps contaminants out that could cause bacteria to grow. Long term storage of water is possible by taking these easy steps.

In the event the water is needed you will be happy you do not have to search for potable water to drink or clean a wound with. If you have a lack of storage space stockpiling water may be difficult. However, making room is a wise investment. If space such as in a small apartment is extremely tight I strongly suggest the filtering straws and mapping out the nearest water source. Local emergency managers should be able to provide information as to what sources of water are the best to use in an emergency.

Heat is another must have item I tackled on my preparation list. Depending upon the climate in your area you may have to plan for the lack of propane, gas, or electricity to heat your home. The homeowner in the southern United States may not have to plan as extensively for the winter months. The majority of the country will have winter temperatures that will freeze pipes in homes and possibly lead to hypothermia. We never know when a disaster could strike so planning for varying temperatures is important. Even traditionally very warm climates can experience cold periods.

After the situation with Hurricane Sandy I realized how lucky I was the storm was not followed by a cold front. The very young are at high risk for hypothermia after a loss of heat in a cold environment. A loss of heat may mean having to evacuate to a warming center or a shelter. Hopefully, you are able to get to one and they are not overcrowded. Remember, when a disaster strikes you will not be the only one that is without heat. Many others that have not prepared will be in search of heat as well and I can imagine the shelters and warming centers might run out of room.

Planning on how to get to a warming center or shelter should be done prior to an emergency. I suggest preparations be made to have alternative sources of heat utilized. This may mean installing a wood burning stove, using a fireplace, or using an electric heater off of a generator. The use of any of these sources should be done with caution and it is important to make sure a fireplace or stove is in good working order and free of any exposures that could catch fire. Be careful not to have any obstructions that could cause carbon monoxide poisoning. Carbon monoxide alarms should already be installed in your home. Online or in a store a carbon monoxide alarm can be bought for around twenty dollars.

Motor vehicles will provide heat as a temporary source. Motor vehicles will not be able to heat your home and the possibility exists that pipes may burst. Knowing how to shut off the water and drain the pipes will definitely pay off should you have to evacuate or have no source of heat for your home. Make sure that if a snow event has occurred the exhaust is free from clogging due to accumulated snow. The exhaust should be able to be vented to an area away from the car to prevent carbon monoxide poisoning. Never operate a vehicle in an enclosed area such as a garage. Dryer vents also need to be cleared after a snow event.

A wood burning stove is a great provider of heat. However, without a wood pile to be fuel for the fire the stove is useless. Knowing how much wood or coal you will need to heat your home is essential. This also depends upon the climate. I have a fireplace and keep enough on hand to get me through two months. I have an additional stockpile nearby that will allow me to add to that supply in the event my generator fails.

Food is a critical area that is essential. We have all seen the empty food shelves that occur at the mention of a storm. The wrong time to go out looking for food is just before or after an emergency hits. Roads may make travel impractical or impossible, and the shelves may be empty. You might luck out and find an adequate supply. This book is all about preparing so that you know you have items you need on hand prior to an incident. I am lucky to have space in my house for a pantry that will sustain us for quite some time. My wife has stocked the pantry with protein bars and canned items. These items taste good and will last a long time. The amount of food required to be stored will depend upon the size of the family or any visitors anticipated. The human body can go a long time without food, however with proper planning food sources that you like can be on hand with a bit of preparation. Protein bars are an excellent food source that can easily be brought with you in a go bag should evacuation be necessary.

Some homes have gone so far as to have plans in place for gardens and growing food for years, or stockpiles of food in order to sustain life for generations. This book is written to help you get through temporary situations and staying alive until help can arrive or other arrangements can be made for long term food sources. Sheltering in place can be made more comfortable by making arrangements to have some food that will not spoil. Should barriers make getting to the store impossible, or keep food suppliers from reaching your local grocery store, you will make it until help arrives.

Having preparations made for the lack of water, heat, and food makes you much better prepared to handle a disaster. Ignoring these items will put you in a bad situation should disaster occur. The cost can be minimal if you plan ahead. Gambling by not having these items in place can lead to unnecessary illness, injury, or death. I strongly suggest you have these items stockpiled and if you do not, then begin today.

Chapter 3

When the Power Goes Out

Electricity is something that all of us take for granted. The ability to flip a switch and have light, pop a meal in the microwave and cook a meal in minutes, and turn on the television are tasks that we assume will always be there. When a small storm strikes and the power goes out for a few hours, or a car strikes a utility pole and we go without electricity for a few hours, we realize the many problems that can accompany not having it. Just walking around the house without bumping into something in the dark becomes an issue.

Are you prepared to handle more than a few hours without power? If the answer is no you should have some preparations made to light your house, power a radio, and perform other tasks.

How reliable is the power grid in your area? You may never need to use the preparations you make in order to make it through without electricity.

Former President Barak Obama issued an executive order on October 13, 2016 in response to warnings regarding the sun and space weather. A portion of the executive order taken from Whitehouse.gov is as follows:

EXECUTIVE ORDER
COORDINATING EFFORTS TO PREPARE
THE NATION FOR SPACE WEATHER EVENTS

By the authority vested in me as President by the Constitution and the laws of the United States of

America, and to prepare the Nation for space weather events, it is hereby ordered as follows:

Section 1. Policy. Space weather events, in the form of solar flares, solar energetic particles, and geomagnetic disturbances, occur regularly, some with measurable effects on critical infrastructure systems and technologies, such as the Global Positioning System (GPS), satellite operations and communication, aviation, and the electrical power grid. Extreme space weather events - those that could significantly degrade critical infrastructure - could disable large portions of the electrical power grid, resulting in cascading failures that would affect key services such as water supply, healthcare, and transportation. Space weather has the potential to simultaneously affect and disrupt health and safety across entire continents. Successfully preparing for space weather events is an all-of-nation endeavor that requires partnerships across governments, emergency managers, academia, the media, the insurance industry, non-profits, and the private sector.

It is the policy of the United States to prepare for space weather events to minimize the extent of economic loss and human hardship. The Federal Government must have (1) the capability to predict and detect a space weather event, (2) the plans and programs necessary to alert the public and private sectors to enable mitigating actions for an impending space weather event, (3) the protection and mitigation plans, protocols, and standards required to reduce risks to critical infrastructure prior to and during a credible threat, and (4) the ability to respond to and recover from the effects of space weather. Executive departments and agencies (agencies) must coordinate their efforts to prepare for the effects of space weather events.

Sec. 2. Objectives. This order defines agency roles and responsibilities and directs agencies to take specific actions to prepare the Nation for the hazardous effects of space weather. These activities are to be implemented in conjunction with those identified in the 2015 National Space Weather Action Plan (Action Plan) and any subsequent updates. Implementing this order and the Action Plan will require the Federal Government to work across agencies and to develop, as appropriate, enhanced and innovative partnerships with State, tribal, and local governments; academia; non-profits; the private sector; and international partners. These efforts will enhance national preparedness and speed the creation of a space-weather-ready Nation.

Former President Obama must have been provided with some evidence pointing to the possibility of a severe space weather event occurring. This executive order defines specific actions. However, as I have pointed out previously, I strongly suggest you do not rely upon the government unless it is absolutely necessary to assist you in running your household after an incident.

Large solar storm events could cause the cascading events described in the executive order. Entire continents with populations in the many millions will be looking for the same resources. It is my opinion the federal government will not be able to provide enough resources in a timely enough manner to provide for millions of effected people. The Amish people that do not rely upon electricity for everyday survival will adjust rather easily, however the majority of the nation, especially in the cities, will have difficulty as the lights go out. Crime is a factor that you should be aware of when the power is out or during any emergency. I will discuss that area of preparation later in the book.

The types of emergencies that we might face are varied and difficult to determine ahead of time. An area that is prone to wildfires should have residents with emergency plans in place for adequate transportation and evacuation routes. An area that is prone to tornadoes should have an adequate shelter to retreat to if persons are unable to get out of the path. Some disasters such as a terror attack or earthquake can occur with no warning and could lead to confusion and difficulty in operating at night.

One of the cheapest and most needed preparations that can be made is to have a flashlight or work light in an emergency kit. The advancements made in flashlights over the past several years have led to much brighter and longer lasting lights. Some of the best lights to have on hand are hand-crank lights that do not require any batteries, and with a one minute crank can have several minutes of use. These lights are bright enough that you could signal for help to let someone know where you are or it could be used to look for others after an incident. The newer lights are not overly expensive and I have tested them over the course of several years and they are reliable so far.

The size of flashlights can vary from very small but powerful to large work lights. Some operate solely on batteries and others work by recharging. The most significant item to remember with these lights is that having a light with no power is useless. I keep in my vehicle and home several types of lights that can be cranked, recharged with an outlet, and powered by C and A cell batteries.

I keep batteries in storage and not in the light as I do not want them to go bad and ruin the light. Installation of batteries into a flashlight is quick and rather easy. Make sure to test the light after purchase by installing the battery and then place the batteries in storage. This makes sure you know how to install the batteries and that the light works. Most big stores carry a variety of lights, including a ten pack of bright LED lights for around ten dollars. The investment in a good emergency light is worth it and if funds allow it a really good led light can be purchased that will last a long time. Batteries can also be purchased in quantities that will allow you to operate a light for days or if used sparingly for weeks. Local stores have the sizes you will need and for a reasonable price you can have sufficient battery storage on hand. Hand crank or battery lanterns have improved greatly as well. Lanterns allow for 360 degrees of light to fill a room. I have found 360 degrees of light gives a feeling of normalcy as opposed to the flashlight pointing to the ceiling to light a room.

Homes can also be equipped with emergency lighting that comes on when the power goes out. This may be needed if you have older family member that needs lighting to keep from tripping or are older yourself. These lights allow you time to locate your emergency kit, possibly light a candle or power up the flashlights that you will use for the duration of the emergency.

A go bag should have a flashlight with extra batteries. In the event evacuation is necessary you do not want to be in the dark without the ability to navigate at night. Assume that power will go out and street lights will not be lit. Using a flashlight will make evacuation easier and provide a manner to signal others. I would not suggest relying upon the light from a cell phone to be the primary light for emergencies or for evacuation. I will discuss communications in the next chapter, but it is smart to not use cell phone lights unless it is for a small period of time to locate a flashlight or the only light available at the time. Cell phones will be needed to use for communications and I do not like to see them used as primary light sources.

A whole house generator is a great way to keep the lights on and recharge flashlights. The type and size of generator you need can be provided by an expert. Some of these generators are able to come on automatically, which is important if your home has a person that is not familiar with generators. These generators can also run on different types of fuel such as propane or a natural gas line. This is a benefit because if you lose one of your sources of fuel to the generator you may have the option of switching to another source. Whatever you decide regarding a generator make sure you have a professional install and inspect the wiring. One of the dangers generators improperly hooked up can cause is sending electricity out to the pole that supplies your house. This could cause severe injury or death to power line workers or others that may be dealing with down power lines.

Another potential source of power is from solar power. I have solar power on the roof of my house. This is an excellent money saver and I enjoy being part of reducing my family carbon footprint. The problem with solar power in my situation is that I do not have a source to store the power with. I either use the power the sun provides in my house or send it out to the grid for others to use. Some kits are available that will allow you to set up a solar panel and, using deep cell batteries, store this electricity for immediate use or for a loss of power. I see potential problems relying upon solar during stormy weather when the sun is not shining. Solar power needs the sun and if the sun is not out you are not making electricity. It would make an excellent longer term solution for extended outages as the sun will eventually come out.

Motor vehicles can be a source of electricity if they are set up with a convertor. I do not suggest this become a long-term solution, as your car will have to be running which burns fuel and a person should be stationed with the auto to keep it from becoming stolen. Convertors can be installed and run off the vehicle or some new cars do have plugs in them as my Chevy Silverado does. The problem you could run into is how much the convertor will be able to run without blowing a fuse. A cigarette plug-in convertor will typically convert 12 volt to 120 volt and provide up to 150 watts. This will charge a cell phone, but is a long way from running much else. Some convertors can run a great deal if properly installed. If this is a route you choose I suggest you research how large of a convertor your car will be able to run and how much that will run.

Additionally, do some calculations on how much gasoline your car will burn while running. This will give you an idea how much fuel you will need on hand. I would rather keep my vehicles with fuel for possible evacuation. This decision like all of my suggestions is up to you.

Chapter 4

Television, Phones, and Communication

An additional area to plan for is how to communicate and obtain information when normal methods are unavailable. I recently watched video from a wildfire that burned many homes in a Tennessee town. Some of the residents reported to the media they had no idea they needed to evacuate and had obtained little information regarding the proximity of the fire. Weather alert radios are a must have in a home emergency kit and are inexpensive to obtain. I purchased a hand crank radio with weather alert for around fifty dollars. This radio will also work on solar power and can be used to charge a cell phone through a USB connection. A weather alert radio will keep you in touch with local radio stations that can keep you updated on the latest information. Information sharing is very important and the more means of communication you have the better off you will be. The weather alert radio voice has been changed over the years to make listening to the station much easier to understand.

I prefer redundancy in my preparation and have satellite television as well as cable Internet. Cable television and satellite signals might both not operate during a serious incident. To plan for that possibility I purchased digital antennae for my televisions. When I point the antennae toward the New York City I receive numerous channels. I receive local weather and news channels without using satellite or cable. These antennae are not very expensive and can be very useful should the more common means of receiving signals fail. Testing these units during a non-emergency will allow you to know what signals are possible to obtain in your geographical area. If you are looking for local channels that your satellite package does not provide, you might obtain these channels with the digital air antennae. A digital convertor may be needed if you have an older model television.

Cell phones are the most common form of communication that almost all of us have on us. Cell phone batteries last for varying amounts of time depending upon the amount of use and other factors, such as applications that are being run. I suggest, during any emergency, switching the setting to battery conservation mode to prolong the amount of battery life. This setting is often found in your phone's settings and apps can also be downloaded that will manage battery life by shutting off background applications that are draining your battery.

Shutting off the phone when it is low and only occasionally turning it on may become necessary if a charging station or other source of power cannot be found. I keep several fully charged portable battery chargers in my home and in my go bag to make sure I have back up sources of power that will last several days if needed. I can also use the hand crank radio and solar radio I mentioned earlier to make sure I always have several sources of power. Cell towers will have several days' worth of back-up power available, so it is possible that cell service may work in the event of a disaster and power loss.

When I was younger, prior to cell phones, one of the ways in which my friends and I communicated was with the use of citizen band radios. They were cheap, relatively easy to install, and as long as the frequency was not overly crowded it was a very effective way to communicate. These systems are still in use today and you can purchase them rather easily online. These radios can be used by plugging them in to a power plug in a car or you can have a professional install them. I like the portability of plugging them in and do not care for an antenna installed on my vehicle. The choice is yours.

Cell phones connected to the internet or any device with internet connection can be a great way to leave messages for others. Some social media sites have ways to notify other you are safe after a crisis.

I suggest you research additional means of radio communications for redundancy. The FCC in the United States regulates the use of radio frequencies. The FCC has a great deal of information on their website that will answer questions you may have regarding licensing. Radios will require licenses to operate on certain frequencies. In my research, I found the Government Mobile Radio Service (GMRS) radio frequency was ideal for my family. A GMRS repeater is located very close to my house. This repeater is located very high and with a small portable radio I can speak with my family members for many miles in each direction. With a very moderate investment, I applied for and obtained a government license to operate on the GMRS frequencies. The license is good for five years and enables my family to use the frequencies as well. Some of these frequencies are set up with repeaters that you can use for free or for a fee. The internet has a website that will let you know what is available in your area. If you decide to use GMRS communication do your research on the restrictions for radio wattage and geographical restrictions that are in place in parts of the country. In rural areas, you may be able to install your own repeater for communications.

Chapter 5

Fire and First Aid

One of the best investments that can be made, and an item that should be in every home, is a fire extinguisher. Depending upon what is burning, a fire can spread in size very quickly. Within minutes a fire can consume an entire home. A properly charged and inspected fire extinguisher could mean the difference between having a small fire and putting it out, and losing everything you have ever owned.

When purchasing a fire extinguisher, I suggest you look for an extinguisher that will be large enough to put out a fire yet not so big that you are unable to operate it. Retail stores sell a basic multi-purpose fire extinguisher for approximately $17.00. I suggest a multipurpose fire extinguisher type ABC which will put out most residential type fires. You can also purchase larger units if needed. Retail websites have a variety of sizes to choose from. The key word to look for is *multi-purpose* when purchasing an extinguisher. These units can be mounted to a wall for easy access. I also suggest keeping an extinguisher in your motor vehicle in the event one is needed. Extinguishers should be inspected for pressure and obstructions on a periodic basis. It is always better to have one and not need it than to need an extinguisher and not have one.

Another area that may require attention in your home is making sure you have functioning smoke detectors. Local fire departments are excellent sources of information on the types of detectors available. A smoke detector is a must in every home and I suggest several, especially if you have a larger home. Testing of smoke detectors should be done regularly. Retail stores carry smoke detectors for as little as $7.00. I have written about the importance of carbon monoxide detectors in another section of the book, however, be aware that retail stores also have combination alarms that detect smoke and carbon monoxide. An extra set of batteries for these alarms is a smart investment. These alarms will last quite a while on battery power, but if an outage is very long you may need to change the battery. Ask your local fire official how many detectors you will need and where to place them.

Fire escape plans should be in place, including areas that a family will meet up should a fire occur. Knowing everyone is evacuated safely is not only important for peace of mind, but it allows responding firefighters to know that everyone is safe. They can concentrate on fighting the fire and not on searching for possible victims that are already safe.

First aid is an area that must be given significant attention in preparing your home for an emergency. I suggest tailoring your plan as your family changes. Your needs for first aid may change. A basic kit and a more robust kit are easy to obtain from your local store. These kits will provide you with items that can really be a life saver. In the event of a large scale incident it may be impossible to quickly obtain first aid due to an over-burdened emergency medical response system.

Bandages and antiseptic wipes are very important in order to keep cuts and abrasions clean. What may seem like a very small cut could turn into a life-threatening infection. Supplies of bandages that are clean and able to be replaced, as well as antibacterial cream are a very wise investment.

Cardio pulmonary resuscitation (CPR) courses are offered in many communities for a nominal fee. This life saving skill is important to know in an emergency. Knowing persons in your neighborhood that have medical training is critical should you require more advanced medical attention and the medical teams in your community are unable to respond.

Families that have loved ones in need of more advanced medical attention should consult with a doctor to determine what will be needed in the event an incident occurs. Having these plans in place prior to an emergency can be helpful and lower stress levels. A wheelchair may be necessary to move an elderly person from a residence. This is an item that should be purchased and stored at your residence prior to an emergency, as finding one after an emergency will be difficult if not impossible.

Medications that are needed may be difficult to obtain. Having these medications ready to go in an emergency is important. A sufficient stock of medications is important to have should a situation arise that prevents timely delivery. Inquire from your local emergency planners if they have a list of persons or a registry of persons with special requirements for incidents. This will make them aware that a person in your home has a disability or will require special considerations for evacuation etc..

Chapter 6

Vehicles and Get Home Bags

In the event an emergency occurs, and you or your loved ones are not home, it may be difficult to get back home. People often work together during emergencies; however, travel could become difficult. It is possible that you or a loved one may have to travel on foot for a period of time in order to get home.

You may be at work or away when a situation develops that requires you to have materials on hand that will help you get back to your house. A backpack is an excellent way to carry needed items that are essential in getting back to your home.

A backpack is a comfortable way to carry water and other items. They come in a variety of sizes to allow for many supplies. What you keep in the backpack is up to you. I strongly suggest you have a bag with water, pen and paper a first aid kit and a flashlight. Bottles can be refilled with water and will keep you hydrated should you have to walk a great distance. How far your work is will determine the other items necessary in your bag.

I also suggest protein bars or similar foods that will give you calories to stay strong and will be able to be stored in the bag for some time. The objective of a go bag is to get you to your home or away from your home in an evacuation, with supplies to keep you going until you reach a destination that will provide longer needed survival items.

An amount of money that will be sufficient for purchasing items or paying for a ride is a smart investment. I also suggest placing items that could be spoiled if they become wet into plastic bags. A radio and flashlight will provide a means of light and a means of obtaining information. Extra batteries or items that work off solar power or by cranking will be smart investments in a go bag. A poncho for repelling rain will take up little room, but should you be caught in a downpour it will keep your clothes dry. Depending upon the time of year and where you are located clothing to stay warm, such as hats and gloves, will be important. Or, if not needed, that clothing space can be used to keep extra water for dry and hot areas.

A map that will show roadways might be needed to get you going in the right direction. Many people commute to work on trains and may not be knowledgeable of the roadways that you have to traverse to get home. A phone with GPS may have this; however, if the phones go down you could get lost.

A portable backup means of communication may be a wise investment. A portable radio mentioned earlier that can transmit on FRS, GMRS, CB or Ham radio frequencies may be a very reliable way to obtain information or contact others. Portable radios that are on the GMRS band can reach another portable radio using a repeater for several miles distance. A user on the other end may have to monitor a radio to receive your transmission. Testing the portable radio with a family member will ensure that should an emergency occur everyone will know what frequency to tune into to listen for someone trying to reach home.

Go bags at residences for quick evacuation is an important and easy way to be prepared and safe. Keeping these bags accessible and well stocked can lower stress and provide needed supplies. Copies of important documents can be kept in the bag should a quick evacuation occur. This is especially important should a quick escape due to fire or tornado be necessary. Fire can destroy a residence, leaving nothing behind. Paperwork and photos that cannot be replaced may be items you wish to keep in your go bag. I am not suggesting that you risk losing valuable evacuation time by going to get the go bag, if time does not allow. The go bag should be readily accessible and if on the way, grab it. Do not lose valuable time searching for the bag or getting the bag if conditions are rapidly getting worse.

Additional items that can be placed into a go bag are ropes, tarps, or other materials that can provide a temporary means of shelter. Weight is of concern when putting together a go bag. You should not put together a bag that will be too heavy to carry, especially if you may have to travel on foot. If you are planning on leaving in a motor vehicle, you should be able to have more materials that can be taken out should travel by vehicle become impossible.

When I recently purchased a motor vehicle, one of the most important factors that went into my decision was safety. I want my wife and children to be as safe as possible. One of the most important lessons I learned while overseeing a traffic bureau as a police officer is that safer vehicles definitely save lives.

Earlier, I discussed a fire that occurred in the woods of Tennessee. I was following this story closely. While viewing video of the persons that became trapped in the wooded areas and escaped unharmed, I came upon a video of two persons escaping the fires through roadways that had been littered with debris and downed trees. I could hear their truck going over trees and other items that I knew they would not have been able to drive over in many small vehicles with low clearance. Although I do not live in a wooded area, the video made enough of an impression on me that I decided the next vehicle purchase I made would be a four wheel drive pickup truck. A truck with room for my family and enough clearance to get over small downed trees or curbs, and that may allow for an avenue of escape that small vehicles cannot get over.

I decided on the Chevy Z71 pickup truck as my choice vehicle. The truck I purchased is a quad cab (4 doors) rated for off-road driving and will allow me to take my family anywhere comfortably. The four-wheel drive will allow for us to get through the snow we get in the Northeast, as well as keep us prepared in the event I have to go off-road, or evacuate and need to carry supplies in the rear of the truck. I strongly suggest making safety your first priority in choosing a new or used vehicle to purchase. Under vehicle clearance was an important for in my purchase. Your evacuation plan may involve mass transit and not a vehicle; however, if it does involve a car, make sure you do your research.

Chapter 7

Pets

My family is lucky and with the help of a friend we adopted the best dog in the world. You will want to keep your pet safe in a crisis as well. People have very strong connections to pets and I believe this is one of the reasons that some people do not evacuate when ordered to, placing the homeowner and the pet in danger. They may not have any plans in place to evacuate their pets or area, afraid they will become separated. This topic is so important to me that I have dedicated a chapter just to this area.

Emergency planners are recognizing the importance of planning for a pet and are becoming more aware of the need to plan for animals during an evacuation or storm. I strongly suggest you investigate if shelters that you may be evacuated to will have the ability to house your pet(s). If they do not determine if pet shelters are nearby so you will have access to them. The plans that you make for you and your family for evacuation should have your pet in mind. Making these plans ahead of time will also allow you to locate locations close to your evacuation point that will have a Veterinarian to assist you if needed.

Those of you that have animals that are larger in size or if you have multiple animals, such as on a farm, you should really have arrangements in place to evacuate them if time allows. A property in another county or state may be a location that you could keep them until your farm recovers, or another area can be located for permanent housing. Whatever your situation is, the time for making arrangements for pets is not during or just after an emergency occurs. You may be placing your life, your family, or your pets' lives in danger, if you do not plan ahead of time.

Many animals have medications that are needed. A place within your go bag can be reserved for these medications. Other items in the go bag that may be required or needed may be paperwork that proves your pet is up to date on rabies shots or similar paperwork. Keeping copies of these items in a plastic bag to protect them and stored in your go bag will save you valuable time.

Pets are very important parts of our lives. Taking a few simple steps to help identify them if they are lost, or assist you in getting them to a safe place in an emergency is a wise investment. Pets will require food and water as well, so remember them when making your extra water on hand calculations. You may have to shelter in place with your pets, so make sure you go to the store and purchase pet food when the supplies are still adequate, but prior to them getting low. Stocking up on pet food is just as important as regular food, so you can enjoy your pet for a long period during a sheltering and keep them well nourished.

Up to date pictures of your pet are important to have in your go bag. This is especially important in the event you become separated or your pet is evacuated from your home while you are away from it.

Copies of photos placed in your go bag will be a back-up in the event your camera or phone is not working to retrieve photos. The last thing you want to have happen is to get into an argument because you cannot retrieve your pet as the shelter attempts to prevent the theft of animals. I would hope that this theft would never occur. When emergencies happen some people look to take advantage of the situation so make sure any shelter has a policy in place and security to prevent the theft of your pet.

In the event that you are away from your home and an incident occurs that would require an evacuation of your pet from the home or building I suggest you plan for a trusted neighbor or friend to be able to retrieve your pet. Make sure that your pet has a collar that has written on it your name and cell phone number should you become separated. Micro-chipping is also available should your pet become separated or stolen and ends up at a veterinarian or shelter that is able to read the information. I mentioned this earlier and it is important enough to again reiterate you will need to keep your pets in mind when calculating how much water to keep stored for a shelter in place. Water and food is essential for your pets just as it is for humans. Warmth and protection from heat is also important for animals so keep this in mind should you lose heat or air conditioning in the home.

Chapter 8

Become Involved

My first introduction to the Community Emergency Response Team (CERT) was a meeting I attended after I was selected to become a Deputy Emergency Management Coordinator in my hometown of Green Brook, New Jersey. I met some of the nicest people, who had volunteered and taken free training through the county emergency management. This enables them to assist in times of emergency. They had taken steps and were given some equipment to be visible and protected should they be activated to assist.

Volunteer CERT team members, volunteer firefighters, and volunteer EMTs are excellent ways to obtain training that will help prepare you to protect your family and others against fire or medical emergencies. This training is often free and many municipalities are in need of volunteers. The CERT training is excellent and does not require as much time as the EMT and firefighting training. I had attended a fire academy prior to the police academy and the training I received in Union County N.J. is excellent. The lessons I learned in fire suppression and first aid are lessons that I will have with me for my lifetime.

Many towns allow you to become volunteers in the various emergency management positions and becoming involved is another great way to better prepare you and your family. These are rewarding positions that allow you to help your neighbors. Careers in this area are also rewarding. In the event your township is not looking for volunteers, you can look to local Red Cross chapters to see if they are looking for volunteers. County CERT teams or State Emergency Management officials may also be looking for volunteers.

The saying "knowledge is power" definitely applies to planning for emergencies in the home. The more you know, the better off you will be, and others will look to you to assist them in preparing their home. You may be able to obtain training by joining local volunteers, and you may be provided with supplies needed in an emergency such as flashlights or hard hats. This will reduce your costs in preparing.

Becoming involved does not only entail joining a volunteer group. Asking your local government to make sure the town is prepared for an emergency is important. The government is designed to work for you and many emergency management professionals are excellent at the jobs they do. The time to make sure they are up to the task is not after an emergency. State and federal planners have really stepped up preparedness efforts over the last few years. Communication among these agencies is getting better all the time.

Information on better preparing your home is available from a variety of sources. Along with my twin brother Edward (current police officer and Marine Corps Veteran) we operate a website www.residentialemergencymanager.com that provides a blog area and links to valuable information on these topics. Subscribing to this site and similar sites will allow you to ask questions in a forum or comment section. Emergency planners love to share ideas and the latest information.

Chapter 9

Security and Street Smarts

As a police officer, I often gave crime prevention recommendations to Residential Emergency Managers during security surveys. Properly securing a residence, lighting, and neighborhood watch programs are all components which can keep you and your family safe every day. Knowing the area you are in and the threats you will face during an emergency is important. When an emergency occurs, it is unfortunate that some people see this as an opportunity to make money and take advantage of others. Be smart and do not become a victim.

Most people will come together and work together when disaster strikes. However, I suggest you trust your instincts should you feel you are being scammed or taken advantage of. The security of a residence is not difficult to increase. If you have a generator, you will want to make sure that it is secure and safe from theft. Make sure locks are secure and working. Motion lights are a great deterrent. Keep in mind no item you own is worth losing your life over. Local and State Police agencies will be working overtime during an emergency to keep you safe. Trust that they will do all that they can to prevent theft, and persons from scamming residences and do all you can to assist them by reporting scammers and suspicious persons.

The question of having a firearm as a part of your residential emergency management plan is something that should not be taken lightly. If you decide as I have, to have a firearm to protect you and your family, I implore you to take a safety course and make sure your firearm is stored according to state and local laws. Make sure that no one can steal it or use it improperly. I carried a firearm and can carry one as a retired law enforcement officer, and know what a responsibility it is. This decision is one that only you can make. Please do extensive research on the type of gun and ammo that is right for your needs. Gun shops can supply you with the information you need. I suggest visiting several of them and ask questions. I have found gun shops will offer excellent advice and will find the right size firearm for you. I settled on the Glock 30S pistol as the go-to firearm in my Residential Emergency Management plan. I carried this firearm as a detective and the larger Glock .45 on patrol. I have found the Glock is very reliable and the .45 bullet will have sufficient stopping power, which I hope to never need to test. A three-gun protection plan, which encompasses a pistol, shotgun, and a rifle, is what I utilize for completing the protection of the residence, as each has a unique purpose. Of course, this increases the cost of the residential emergency plan significantly. Properly stored firearms that are taken care of will become part of your next generation's emergency management plan. If you take care of them, they can be passed down to your children, as I will do one day.

If you decide against the use of a firearm as part of your residential emergency management plan, that is fine. Not everyone is comfortable with firearms and if you do not feel that this is the right route for you, I will not think less of you. The security of your home can be increased in other ways, such as increasing security lighting that will work off solar power in the event power goes out. If you are on a generator, the system can be set up to work the exterior lighting of the residence. Partnering with a neighbor that owns a firearm in the event you are in need of protection may be part of your plan.

Police Departments, Sheriff Offices and other law enforcement agencies will send out notices during an emergency or evacuation notifying those who decide to try to scam others, gouge prices, and engage in crimes during times of emergency will face stiff penalties. These messages are important to keep crime down and I believe these press releases work well. Should you find yourself in an emergency situation and have not seen a press release, phone your local law enforcement and ask them to put one out. Getting the word out regarding strict enforcement may be the deterrent that keeps you and your possessions safe.

A positive attitude can keep your spirits high and make you much safer. When emergencies occur, and should disaster strike, working with each other is the best solution to keeping everyone safe. Some people will have emergency plans in place that are designed not to allow anyone else to have anything that they have. That is an unfortunate reality. Should you find yourself in contact with someone that is not willing to share or offer any assistance to you, I suggest you move along and look elsewhere for help. As unfortunate as it is, some people are only concerned with their own welfare. I am confident that you will find many others that will share, offer assistance, and lend a helping hand when needed. During emergencies, an opportunity presents itself to really show how we can help each other. After an incident normalcy will return and people will remember who was kind and who was not. I wish you the best of luck to you in your new role as a Residential Emergency Manager.

Sources

CNN Library - Hurricane Sandy Fast Facts:
www.cnn.com/2013/07/13/world/americas/hurricane-sandy-fast-facts/

The White House, Office of the Press Secretary - Executive Order -- Coordinating Efforts to Prepare the Nation for Space Weather Events:
www.whitehouse.gov/the-press-office/2016/10/13/executive-order-coordinating-efforts-prepare-nation-space-weather-events